BanKing

By Linda Crotta Brennan

Illustrated by Rowan Barnes-Murphy

The Child's World®

Published by The Child's World®
1980 Lookout Drive • Mankato, MN 56003-1705
800-599-READ • www.childsworld.com

Acknowledgments
The Child's World®: Mary Berendes, Publishing Director
The Design Lab: Design and production
Red Line Editorial: Editorial direction

Design elements: Eric Krouse/Dreamstime

ISBN 9781614732396
LCCN 2012932816

Printed in the United States of America
Mankato, MN
July 2012
PA02122

About the Author

Linda Crotta Brennan has a master's degree in early childhood education. She has taught elementary school and worked in a library. Now, she is a full-time writer. She enjoys learning new things and writing about them. She lives with her husband and goofy golden retriever in Rhode Island. She has three grown daughters.

About the Illustrator

Rowan Barnes-Murphy has created images and characters for children's and adults' books. His drawings have appeared in magazines and newspapers all over the world. He's even drawn for greeting cards and board games. He lives and works in Dorset, in southwest England, and spends time in rural France, where he works in an ancient farmhouse.

Mia and Tomás had just finished another busy day at their lemonade stand. They were at Tomás's house for an afternoon snack.

"Here's what we made today at the lemonade stand," said Mia. She handed Tomás his half of the money.

"We did really well!" Tomás exclaimed. He headed to his bedroom with the money.

Mia followed Tomás. In his room, Tomás keeps three jars on a shelf. Each one has a different label: Spend, Give, and Save. He put money in each jar, but the Save jar was too full. The money popped out and fell to the floor.

"You should put your money in a bank," said Mia. "That's what I do."

"I don't know," said Tomás doubtfully. "I thought I'd just get a bigger jar."

"Remember when your dog ate the $10 bill you got for your birthday?" she asked. "And what about that time your little brother took money out of your jar? He spent it on candy. Your money will be safer in a bank."

Tito, Tomás's uncle, knocked on Tomás's door. He had a plate with slices of apple and cheese. "Here's a snack for you," he said, setting the plate on Tomás's desk. "I heard what Mia suggested, Tomás. It's a good idea."

"What if the bank is robbed?" asked Tomás.

"Banks have **insurance**," Uncle Tito explained. "If your bank is robbed or goes out of business, you'll still get your money."

The Federal **Deposit** Insurance Corporation, or FDIC, is an insurance program for banks. It is run by the US government. It protects people's bank accounts up to $250,000.

"And the bank will pay you for keeping your money there," said Mia. "The payment is called **interest**."

Tomás perked up. "That sounds good. How much will the bank pay?"

"Interest rates change," explained Uncle Tito. "But they are a percentage, or part, of your savings."

Tomás picked up his Save jar. "I'll ask Mom if we can go to her bank so I can open an account."

The amount of interest a bank account earns depends on how much money is in the account. For example, 1% interest on $100 is $1. So, if you have $100 in a savings account, you will have $101 after one year without depositing any more money.

The next day, Tomás and his mother drove to Cozy Credit Union. On the way, they passed Bountiful Bank and City Savings and **Loan**. "I never realized there were so many places to keep money," said Tomás. "Is a credit union the same as a bank?"

"Credit unions offer accounts and loans like banks do," explained Tomas's mom. "A big difference is that a credit union is a cooperative. That means it's owned by and run for its members. Often, credit unions pay higher interest rates and charge lower **fees** than banks."

"Is that why you chose Cozy Credit Union?" asked Tomás.

"It is," she said. "Plus, it's easy to get to, and the people are helpful and friendly."

Tomás's mother told a teller Tomás wanted to open a savings account. The teller showed them to an office. A woman greeted Tomás and his mother. "Hello, I'm Mrs. Russo. How may I help you?"

"Hi. I'm Tomás," replied Tomás. "I want to open a savings account."

"I can help you with that," she said. "Please follow me."

The three went into Mrs. Russo's office. Tomás put his jar of money on her desk.

The National Credit Union Administration, or NCUA, is an insurance program for credit unions. It is run by the US government. It protects people's credit union accounts up to $250,000.

"It looks like you are very good at saving," said Mrs. Russo. "Let's open an account for that money. I need some information about you."

Tomás told her his name, birth date, address, and telephone number. Next, Tomás's mom handed Mrs. Russo a card with his Social Security number on it.

"What's that?" Tomás asked.

"It's a number from the US government that only you have," his mom explained. "The number helps identify you. I requested the number when you were born."

Mrs. Russo completed the form. Next, she had Tomás sign it and write the date.

Then, Mrs. Russo counted Tomás's money. "You have $39," she said, writing in a little book. She handed the booklet to Tomás.

"What's this for?" Tomás asked. He opened it. "It says $39, today's date, and $39 again."

"This is your **passbook**," explained Mrs. Russo. "It's also called a bankbook. This is to help you keep track of your deposits and **withdrawals**. These are types of transactions. Every time you make a transaction, note it in your passbook. Note the **balance** that results from the transaction, too."

"So, that's why you wrote $39 twice," Tomás said, looking at the book. "Once for the deposit and once for the balance."

"That's right," Tomás's mom said.

"So, can I take money out of my savings account whenever I want?" asked Tomás.

"Sure," said Mrs. Russo. "It's your money. Your mom just has to come with you."

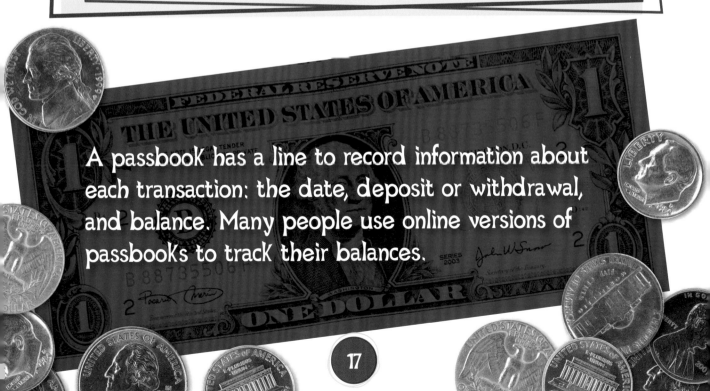

A passbook has a line to record information about each transaction: the date, deposit or withdrawal, and balance. Many people use online versions of passbooks to track their balances.

The next week, Mia and Tomás made $8 selling lemonade. Mia's dad drove them to the bank to deposit their money.

"What happens to the money we deposit?" Mia asked.

"The bank keeps part of the money at the bank," said Mia's dad. "But it puts most of the money to work."

"How can money work?" asked Tomás.

Mrs. Russo heard Tomás's question. "That's a great question, Tomás" she said. "We combine your money with the money from our other savers. We lend this money to people who need it."

"Like when we bought our house," Mia's dad explained. "We took out a loan from the bank to buy it."

"People borrow money to do all kinds of things," Mrs. Russo explained. "They borrow to help pay for college, fix their house, or open a business. That's how banks earn money."

"A bank is a business, just like your lemonade stand," said Mia's dad. "Banks don't lend money for free. They charge interest. Banks pay their savers some of the interest. The rest is profit for the bank."

"What if the people who take out loans can't pay them back?" asked Tomás.

"There's always some risk in lending money," said Mrs. Russo. "Banks check borrowers carefully. For example, do they pay their bills on time? If the bank doesn't think someone will be a dependable borrower, it won't lend money to that person."

"I want to be dependable," said Mia.

"Me, too," added Tomás. "Let's start by depositing our money."

Tomás and Mia each deposited $4 in their savings accounts. Tomás made sure to make an entry in his passbook. He had $43 in his account now.

Tomás grinned. "It's great to be a saver!"

Glossary

balance (BAL-uhns): This is the amount of money in a bank account. When Tomás opened his savings account, he had a balance of $39.

deposit (di-PAH-zit): To put money into a bank account is to deposit it. Mia and Tomás deposited earnings from their lemonade stand into their bank accounts.

fee (FEE): Money charged for a service is a fee. Tomás's mother chose to bank at Cozy Credit Union because it charges the lowest fees.

insurance (in-SHOOR-uhns): This service gives money to a person or business if an accident or theft occurs. The FDIC is a special insurance program that guarantees customers will not lose their savings if their bank is robbed.

interest (IN-trist): Interest is the percentage of money paid on a loan or earned in a savings account. Uncle Tito paid 8% interest on his loan and Mia earned 1% interest on her savings.

loan (LOHN): Money someone borrows from a bank is a loan. Mia's parents took out a loan to buy their house.

passbook (PAS-buk): This is a booklet from the bank in which a customer enters information about savings account transactions. Each time Tomás deposited money into his account, he made an entry in his passbook.

withdrawal (with-DRAW-uhl): To take money out of a bank account is to make a withdrawal. Mia made a withdrawal from her savings account to buy a new bike.

Books

Armentrout, David, and Patricia Armentrout. *The Bank*. Westminster, CA: Teacher Created Resources, 2011.

Johnston, Marianne. *Let's Visit the Bank*. New York: Rosen, 2003.

Rau, Dana Meachen. *What Is a Bank?* New York: Gareth Stevens, 2010.

Web Sites

Visit our Web site for links about banking:

childsworld.com/links

Note to Parents, Teachers, and Librarians: We routinely verify our Web links to make sure they are safe and active sites. So encourage your readers to check them out!

Index